City Shapes

Stars

By Jennifer S. Burke

Welcome
Books

Children's Press
A Division of Grolier Publishing
New York / London / Hong Kong / Sydney
Danbury, Connecticut

Photo Credits: Cover, p. 17, 19 by Nelson Sa; p. 5, 15 by Angela Booth; p. 7, 9 © Indexstock; p.11 © Corbis; p. 13 © Image Bank
Contributing Editor: Mark Beyer
Book Design: Michael DeLisio

Visit Children's Press on the Internet at:
http://publishing.grolier.com

Cataloging-in-Publication Data

Burke, Jennifer S.
    Stars / by Jennifer S. Burke.
      p. cm. — (City shapes)
    Includes bibliographical references and index.
    Summary: Simple text and pictures of everyday objects
introduce star shapes.
    ISBN 0-516-23079-4 (lib. bdg.) — ISBN 0-23004-2 (pbk.)
    1. Stars (Shape) — Juvenile literature [1. Stars
(Shape)] I. Title. II. Series
    QA482.B92 2000   00-031748
    516'.5—dc21

Contents

There are many shapes to see on my street.

There are circles, squares, and rectangles.

Can you find the star?

Some stars light up.

They look **bright** at night.

How many stars do you see?

7

Sometimes you can see a star on the ground.

How many **points** does the star have?

GRETA GARBO

At the **circus** you can look for stars.

Stars can show up anywhere!

How many stars do you count on this ball?

11

This **statue** stands on top of a big star.

Stars can have many points.

13

This wall has stars on it.

What color is the wall?

What color are the stars?

15

I draw stars on the **sidewalk**.

How many stars did I draw?

17

There are stars on the left.

There are stars on the right.

How many stars do you see around this door?

Stars can be many sizes.

Stars in the city are everywhere.

GRETA GARBO

New Words

bright (**bryt**) full of light

circus (**sir**-kus) a show with wild
animals and clowns

points (**poynts**) sharp edges

sidewalk (**syd**-walk) the part of a
street where people walk

statue (**stach**-oo) a shape made
from stone

To Find Out More

Books
I Like Stars
by Margaret Wise Brown
Golden Books Family Entertainment

I See Shapes
by Marcia Fries
Creative Teaching Press

Shapes, Shapes, Shapes
by Tana Hoban
Greenwillow Books

Index

About the Author

Jennifer S. Burke is a teacher and a writer living in New York City. She holds a master's degree in reading education from Queens College, New York.

Reading Consultants

Kris Flynn, Coordinator, Small School District Literacy, The San Diego County Office of Education

Shelly Forys, Certified Reading Recovery Specialist, W.J. Zahnow Elementary School, Waterloo, IL

Peggy McNamara, Professor, Bank Street College of Education, Reading and Literacy Program